I M P R E S   O F

D0834103

Photographs by

Liam Blake

Introduction by **Seán Lucy**

Appletree Press

First published by
The Appletree Press Ltd,
7 James Street South, Belfast
BT2 8DL, 1987

British Library Cataloguing in
Publication Data
Blake, Liam
    Impressions of Cork.
    1. Cork (County)
    —Description and travel
    —Views
    I. Title
    941.9'50824'0222
    DA990.C79
    ISBN 0-86281-193-7

9 8 7 6 5 4 3 2 1

Printed in Ireland

I n t r o d u c t i o n

WHEN you say 'Cork' you say many things. You say Cork city: second city of the Republic of Ireland, third city of the island of Ireland, capital of the province of Munster, nestling at the eastern end of the deep rich valley of the river Lee: a seaport, a merchant and market town; a small, warm, varied urban world.

You say county Cork — but that must be subdivided.

You say East Cork: rich rolling farmland of substantial quiet country towns and villages, where parkland trees and long demesne walls mark the departed dominance of big house and castle.

You say North Cork: its richer land, along the stately Blackwater and opening north into the Golden Vale, is not unlike the east, but altered by the encroachment of high country, of a wilder more Gaelic mode with the Nagle Mountains, the Kilworth Mountains, the Ballyhoura Hills, Slieve Luachra, and round into the Boggeragh Mountains.

You say West Cork, but that again is divided between the high hills, wild mountains, deep valleys, and long bays of the true West; and the coastal territory and gentler farmland running from Cork Harbour west as far as Roaringwater Bay.

All this is the biggest county in Ireland: Ireland's Yorkshire, or perhaps Ireland's Texas. In any case, one of the most various counties and one of the richest in every sense; one of the warmest, and certainly one of the wettest. All of Cork is washed from the south-west. It dozes and drips in the big Atlantic Gulf Stream. The clear soft light is almost submarine. The weather mellows and melts everything. This landscape digests abandoned houses, leaving only softened skeletons of stone. Given half a chance, mould, moss, nettle, fern, bramble, elder, sycamore, heather and gorse take over house, garden and field, with a soft inexorability recalling the great Munster oak forests which once covered so much of the territory.

Even a glance at a small map of Ireland will show the geological shape of the south-west, the structure and texture of the Cork-Kerry massif. The high country runs essentially east to west and west-south-west. In East Cork these red sandstone ridges, these soft Devonian foldings, form rolling hills of fine farming land. As you move west the ridges rise and rise, shouldering up into mountains which thrust their long rocky fingers into the prevailing counterthrust of the big Atlantic weather, and thus form the long deep bays of West Cork and Kerry. Going the other way, running east between the inland ridges, are the three principal rivers of county Cork, the Blackwater, the Lee, and the Bandon. Each of these eventually turns south, passing at right angles through the hills to meet the sea.

Cork county is an English administrative invention dating back, in its present form, to the end of the Elizabethan wars, and made up of lands confiscated from Norman Irish and Gaelic Irish alike.

Yet the county has a certain cohesion, and a very definite psychological identity. Physically it is four ridges rising west and three rivers running east. To the south the ocean; to the west the Atlantic again, and the high watershed of the Cork-Kerry border. The northern borders are vaguer, blending into Kerry, Limerick, and Tipperary in high and low lands up from the Blackwater valley. The Blackwater system also defines the eastern boundaries, though Waterford holds a large fertile triangle in the elbow of the river.

It is from Cork city that the county takes its name. An early version of that name is Corcach Mór

Mumhan, the Great Marsh of Munster. This marsh was an island, or system of islands, formed at the bottom of the valley where salt tide and freshwater met. Today it is the built-over centre of Cork. Corkonians refer to it as 'the flat of the city', and part of it is still called, in English, 'the Marsh'. Through the centuries Cork city has expanded up and down the river valley, and climbed the steep hills to north and south so that it now has the pleasant aspect of a hill town. St Finbarr's monastic site, Viking settlement, Anglo-Norman stronghold and merchant city, market and principal south-western port to the West of England, the Continent and later America, it has been for a thousand years or so, in its own private ways, a small but not insignificant melting-pot for things and people — native and imported.

Apart from the city, Cork county has many substantial and interesting towns. Though most have their own particular flavours, one might trace a generic division. There are settler towns with a strong atmosphere of mixed Anglo-and-Irish heritage; and there are market towns where the older Irish country stock have created a different ambience, almost a village or townland atmosphere, in which the Anglo-Irish heritage would seem alien or at best exotic. With some exceptions, the division, not surprisingly, is a line running south-west through the mid-county. To select, without offence, some examples of the different sorts of town is easy: Youghal, Mallow, and Kinsale illustrate the first kind of town; Millstreet, Macroom, and Bantry the second.

The landscape holds older memories than the towns. Wave after wave of prehistoric people adventured out to, or were driven into, this corner of Europe. Standing stones, forts and cooking wells mark their presence — and the first Munster names in Ogham script. In early Irish legend the south-west is always different: mysterious and even dangerous. It had its own magic, and was perhaps not Celticized in the same way as other parts. St Patrick blessed it from Cashel but never came farther. Cork saints, like Finbarr of the Lee and Gobnait of Ballyvourney, are very local. The Vikings may have founded a war and trade base in Cork itself, but left little mark, except, perhaps, in voices and faces. The Normans on the other hand drove the Eoghanacht kings, MacCarthys and O'Sullivans and others, into the hills and woods. Normans, like FitzGeralds and Barrys, settled down and blended in. East and North Cork are full of their castles. They could not crack West Cork and Kerry whence the resurgent MacCarthys pushed back at them: using new fighting methods and Norman-style building. Blarney Castle is the finest MacCarthy tower-house, only four miles from Norman Cork. Norman and Gael built abbeys and friaries. Intermarriage became as common as raid and feud.

Serious English colonialism swept away all these local princes. Big houses and Protestant churches mark the landlord centuries; parochial houses and Catholic chapels show the more recent rise of the Catholic majority.

In spite of the rich diversity of racial and geographical factors, it must be concluded that the city and the territory of Cork have some strong, digestive, homogenizing power which produces what the rest of Ireland, at least, recognizes, with reactions varying from exasperation to affection, as 'the Cork character'. Cork people are variously described by others as 'bumptious', 'cocky', 'ridiculously self-satisfied', 'smug', 'stubbornly opinionated', 'restless', 'pushy'. There is the old Dublin legend of the continuous Cork invasion of the capital. Getting off the train at Kingsbridge/Heuston each Corkonian throws a penny into the Liffey vowing that if it floats they will go home. There is also the tale of the guide in Milan, praising the glories of its cathedral, who was interrupted by an insistent sing-song voice asking, patronizingly, whether he had seen the Commercial Bank in Cork.

These other-Irish reactions are based on realities of local character. Elsewhere I have tried to describe the Cork character as 'a sort of up-beat Irishness; very refreshing in comparison to some forms of Irish poor-mouth post-colonial *triste*; but also potentially brash and irritating in its insistence, right or wrong, on self-assertion'.

The whole of Munster, of the South-West, shares what can only be described as a soft toughness, and in Cork, city and county, there is a local version of this which I call 'the Cork challenge'. Whether on the hurling field when the red and white Cork colours ('blood and bandages') are flying finely, or in the bar when a powerful statement is interrupted by a keen glance, a raised hand, and the fatally polite words, 'Excuse me now! Hold on a second there. Am I correct in asserting that you maintain . . . ?' — everywhere, in politics, in business, in law, in conversation, and in sport, the Cork challenge is heard and enjoyed. No people seem at once so convivial and so competitive. When Cork people are having a splendid discussion, English visitors often think a deadly quarrel is in progress.

The taproot of what is perceived, particularly by outsiders, as the Cork character is the fact that almost all Cork people are sincerely pleased and

9

proud to be Cork people. It is not being suggested that such pride and pleasure is not felt in other Irish counties; but in the pride and pleasure of Cork is a solid assumption that, in many ways, Cork city and county are as good as or better than anything in Ireland; and, given a modicum of luck and money, the only place that any sane person would chose to live. This self-confidence and self-satisfaction can be found in local variety from the West Cork Gaeltacht to the solid merchant and professional suburbs of Cork city, and give, at best, a snug, solid sense of comfort.

Yet, in spite of this warm and sometimes maddening self-satisfaction, Cork is very open to the outer world, in many ways more so than Dublin. 'Cork loves a stranger', goes the old saying, and the bright good manners of most Cork people are a pleasure. The term 'good manners', though, is used deliberately, because some visitors or settlers, coming from colder, less courteous societies, mistake these easy chatty good manners for real regard, or even for deep affection. This is simply a misreading of signs. Except in parts of Ulster where strangers get the impression that they are liked *less* than they are, this happens all over Ireland; but nowhere more than in Cork. It is *rude* in Cork not to treat other people as if they were your friends. It is *rude* to address anyone without smiling. This does not mean that everyone is a friend, or even that they are really pleased to see you.

When Cork people are pleased to see each other, or the welcome stranger, it is often largely for the stimulation. They are easily bored and endlessly curious, particularly about the foibles and freaks of human behaviour.

This sounds cold; but, though they are not quite the charming warm people they seem to some visitors, yet there is often, below good-manners, below sentimentality and cynicism, a secret, steady Cork kindness and generosity, which, oddly enough, is almost ashamed of itself.

When a Cork aquaintance knows you well enough to be comfortably rude to you, you will know that you are accepted.

SEÁN LUCY

Sunrise over Bantry Bay ➤

Misty morning, Kinsale ➤
(overleaf)

◄ Buoys, Kinsale

Windows, Kinsale

Windows, Cork city

Cork city docks

River Lee, Cork city

St Finbarr's Cathedral, ➤
Cork city

Steps, Cork city

Shandon and river Lee,
Cork city

Eyeries, West Cork ►

Kenmare bay from the
Beara peninsula

West Cork landscape

Cottage door, near Mallow

Shopfront, West Cork ➤

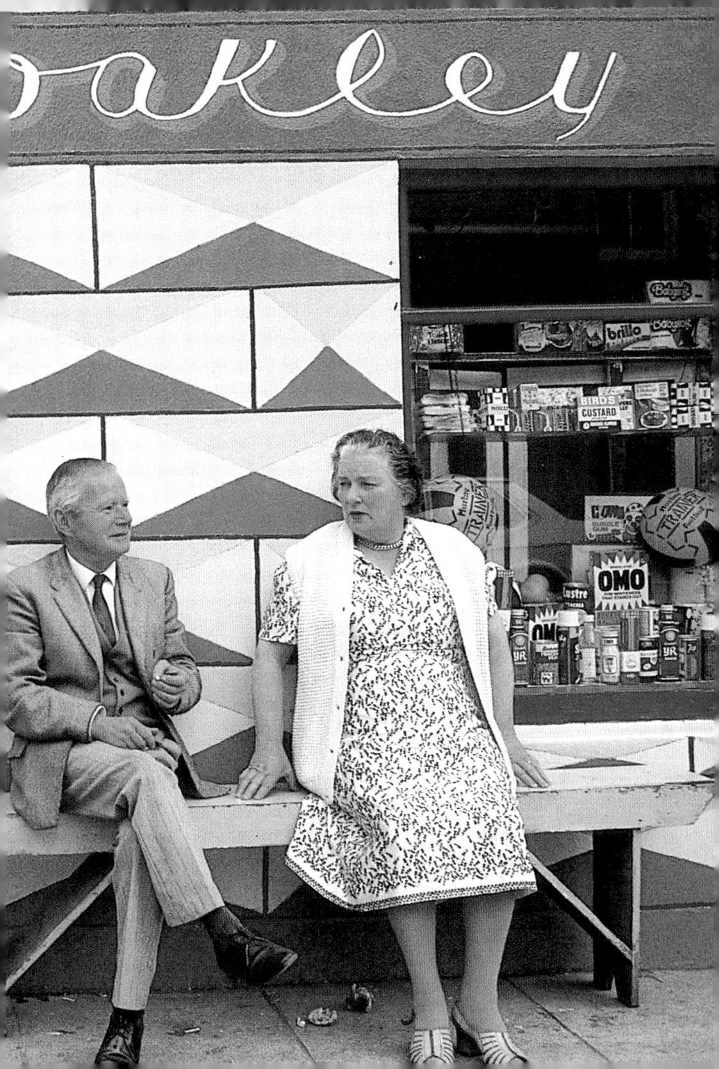
oakley
brillo
BIRD'S
CUSTARD
TRAINER
OMO
Lustre

Near Allihies, West Cork

Blarney Castle ►

Near Dursey island

Dursey island ➤

Eyeries village

Eyeries (overleaf) ➤

In the Beara peninsula ➤

◀Stone circle, Ardgroom

Bull lighthouse at sunset ➤
(overleaf)

Pub and former booking
office for the *Lusitania*,
Allihies

Allihies at sunset ➤

St Finbarr's
Cathedral at
night

◄ Sunset at Bally-
donegan strand,
West Cork